Matters of Opinion

BULLYING

BY
CARLA MOONEY

NORWOODHOUSE PRESS
CHICAGO, ILLINOIS

Norwood House Press
P.O. Box 316598
Chicago, Illinois 60631

For information regarding Norwood House Press, please visit our website at:
www.norwoodhousepress.com or call 866-565-2900.

LIBRARY OF CONGRESS CATALOGING-IN-PUBLICATION DATA

Mooney, Carla.
  Bullying / by Carla Mooney.
     pages cm. -- (Matters of opinion)
  Includes bibliographical references and index.
  Summary: "Explores pros and cons of several issues related to bullying
including; who's to blame, prevention programs, and punishments. Aligns with
Common Core Language Arts Anchor Standards for Reading Informational Text
and Speaking and Listening. Text contains critical thinking components for social
issues and history. Includes bibliography, glossary, index, additional resources and
instructions for writing an opinion-based essay"-- Provided by publisher.
   ISBN 978-1-59953-754-2 (library edition : alk. paper) -- ISBN 978-1-60357-862-2
(ebook)
  1. Bullying in schools--Juvenile literature. I. Title.
   LB3013.3.M66 2016
   371.5'8--dc23
                                                          2015027481

289N—062016
Manufactured in the United States of America in Brainerd, Minnesota.

Contents

Note: Words that are **bolded** in the text are defined in the glossary.

Timeline

1838   The first use of *bullying* appears in a literary work, *Oliver Twist*, written by Charles Dickens.

1970   Dr. Dan Olweus begins systematic research on bullying and its effects. His research is published in Sweden in 1973 and in the United States in 1978.

1998   Matthew Shepard, a 21-year-old, dies after being tied to a fence and tortured by anti-gay bullies.

1999   High school students Eric Harris and Dylan Klebold shoot students at Columbine High School in Littleton, Colorado, killing 13 and wounding more than 20 others before killing themselves.

1999   Georgia becomes the first state to pass anti-bullying legislation that requires schools to have policies that define bullying and procedures to investigate and punish bullying incidents.

2000   Cyberbullying incidents increase with the growth of Internet and digital technologies.

2001   The National Education Association reports that more than 160,000 students skip school every day to avoid being bullied by other students.

2002   A report released by the US Secret Service and the US Department of Education concludes that bullying played a significant role in many school shootings.

2003   Thirteen-year-old Ryan Halligan hangs himself at home after being relentlessly bullied at school and online.

2005   The STOMP Out Bullying program is created by Ross Ellis. The major goal of the program is to effectively reduce bullying and its various forms, such as cyberbullying.

2006   Megan Meier, a 13-year-old, commits suicide after being bullied online with a fake Myspace social network profile.

2006   The US Congress passes a law making it a federal crime to annoy, abuse, threaten, or harass another person over the Internet.

2008   California passes one of the first cyberbullying laws, which gives school officials the authority to discipline students for bullying others off campus or online.

2010   Tyler Clementi, an 18-year-old college student, commits suicide after being cyberbullied.

2011   New Jersey passes one of the country's harshest bullying laws to date, which requires all bullying cases to be reported to the state.

2015   Forty-nine states have anti-bullying legislation and/or policies in place.

1 The Bullying Problem

For Johnny Cagno, an eighth grader at Birchwood Middle School in North Providence, Rhode Island, school was a nightmare. "I wasn't accepted at school. I couldn't be who I am. . . . I was very, very scared to go to school every day," he says. Growing up, Johnny was not interested in typical "boy" activities like playing sports or hanging with the guys. Instead, he enjoyed making costumes for a play or spending time with girls. He says his differences made him a target for bullies. "Growing up, you play sports. If you don't play sports, then you're weird or, you know, you just don't fit in," he says. "And all through my life, that's how it's been. I don't fit in."[1]

Johnny started seventh grade at Birchwood in 2009. By then bullying had already pushed him out of two other schools. He hoped that he would have a fresh start at Birchwood. But the bullying continued. Increasingly, the

Bullying can have long-lasting effects on the person bullied.

bullying took a toll on Johnny. He began to cut himself. His mother, Lisa, says Johnny repeatedly told her that he hated himself and that he did not want to live anymore. No matter what she did, she could not get those feelings out of his mind.

So Lisa called Birchwood officials for help. Liz Vachon is the school's social worker. She says Johnny's case was a wake-up call for the school. "His case was the case that changed everything," she says. "That was the point when I recognized that this is really serious. . . . It's the first time,

What Causes Bullying?

Bullying takes place for many reasons. But some studies show it has common triggers. Many bullies act out to get attention from peers, parents, or teachers. They might use bullying to get what they want or to be accepted by a group of peers. Sometimes kids who feel inadequate bully to make themselves feel important or cool. Other times, bullies who are feeling frustration, anger, or pain in another part of their lives try to express these feelings by hurting others. "In fact, bullies are often not focused on those they bully at all. They just want to feel better about themselves by making someone else, anyone else, feel worse," says Nailah Coleman. She is a doctor at Children's National.

Quoted in Children's National Health System, "Do Social Media and the Internet Make Bullying Worse?," October 28, 2013.

really, I had parents coming in asking for help on their child's behalf." She began speaking out about bullying, holding assemblies, and talking to students. "We have to do something system wide," she says. And once she started talking about bullying, she suddenly saw the true scope of the problem as more students came forward to report incidents. "It went from 30 percent of bullying to about 70 percent of bullying cases coming forward,"[2] she says.

Many Forms of Bullying

In the United States, stories like Johnny's are common. The National Center for Educational Statistics says nearly one in three students report being bullied during the school year. *Bullying* is defined as unwanted, aggressive behavior. It involves a real or perceived power imbalance. Sometimes bullying is a one-time event. Often it happens many times over a period of weeks, months, or even years.

Recent studies have proven that bullied young people are not mentally healthy in their adult lives.

Bullying actions take many forms. Some are easier to see than others. In some cases bullying is physical. It can include hitting, kicking, pinching, spitting, tripping, and pushing, damaging possessions, or making mean gestures. Other times, bullying is verbal. Bullies tease, call names, make sexual comments, or threaten victims. And in some cases bullying is harder to see. Bullies may gossip behind a person's back. They may spread rumors on the Internet or leave someone out of plans on purpose. This type of social bullying is meant to hurt a person's reputation or relationships with others. It inflicts emotional damage on victims.

Bullying is not just a school problem. It can happen at any time and in any place. It can take place at school or after school, on the bus, and at the playground. It can even happen at home, through the phone, computer, and Internet.

Cyberbullying

More kids use cell phones and the Internet today than in the past. And cyberbullying has emerged as a new way to hurt others. It uses technology such as cell phones,

Bullies Are Impacted, Too

Bullying impacts everyone involved. This includes the bullies themselves. The US Department of Health and Human Services has an anti-bullying website. It says kids who bully others are more likely to abuse alcohol and drugs as teens and adults. Experts say that bullies may be more likely to use alcohol or drugs because they are trying to self-medicate and escape their own problems. They are also more likely to get into fights, vandalize property, and get in trouble with the law. The trouble does not end with adolescence. It can follow them into adulthood. Adults who were bullies are more likely to be abusive to partners, spouses, and kids. One 2008 study completed with the cooperation of New York University and Queens University gave a hint as to why. It found that kids who bully are more likely to have conflicts in relationships with parents and friends. They are also more likely to lack social and problem-solving skills.

Bullies are more likely to have alcohol and drug abuse problems as teens and adults.

Bullies have started using the Internet to harass their victims.

computers, and tablets. On the Internet, the bullying takes place on social media sites, chat rooms, and websites. For instance, bullies send threats in text messages or e-mails. They spread rumors in chat rooms and on social media. Bullies also post or share embarrassing pictures and videos of victims. In some cases they create entire websites or fake social media profiles to embarrass and threaten victims. The American Academy of Pediatrics says cyberbullying is the most common online risk for all teens.

Cyberbullying can be very hurtful. It can happen at any time or any place. It can even reach kids at home. As a result, kids who experience cyberbullying have a hard time getting away from it. It can also be anonymous. Instead of face-to-face confrontations, bullies can post messages while hiding their identities behind a computer screen. These can spread to a large number of people very quickly. Cyberbullying can also be long lasting. Victims often find it hard to delete harassing or embarrassing messages.

Impact of Bullying

Bullying affects everyone—bullies, victims, and the people who see it. It can have serious negative effects on kids' education, health, and safety. Those who are bullied are more likely to avoid school and be absent. The National Education Association says about 160,000 kids a day stay home from school to avoid being bullied. When at school, bullied students have a hard time concentrating. And they are less interested in doing well at school. As a result, these students are more likely to have poor grades and drop out of school.

In many cases a person who is bullied may feel isolated or alienated. In a small number of cases, these feelings can lead them to harm themselves or others. They may cut themselves or turn to drugs or alcohol to escape the bullies. And in some cases bullied kids have attempted suicide. Johnny Cagno says that at one point he believed suicide was the only way to escape the bullies. "They got inside my head," he says. "I would say, 'If I kill myself, I don't have to deal with this, you know. I won't have [to] deal with the bullies every day.'"[3] One day while he was at home alone, Johnny took an overdose of cold pills. After taking the pills, he called his father and told him what he had done. Johnny's father rushed him to the hospital, where he recovered from the suicide attempt. He has since decided not to return to school and plans to finish middle school at home.

In a few cases bullied kids have used violent means to strike back. This was the case with high school students Eric Harris and Dylan Klebold. They were both bullied at school. One day in 1999, they brought guns to school. They shot students at Columbine High School in Littleton, Colorado. They killed 13 and wounded more than 20 others before

Thousands of children stay home or avoid school in order to escape bullies.

killing themselves. In cases like this, the devastating impact of bullying is felt by an entire community.

A Look Inside This Book

The bullying debate is complex and hard to discuss. In this book three issues will be covered in more detail: Has the Internet made bullying worse? Are schools doing enough to stop bullying? Should bullying be a criminal offense? Each chapter ends with a section called **Examine the Opinions**, which highlights one argumentation technique used in the chapter. At the end of the book, students can test their skills at writing their own essay on the book's topic. Finally, notes, a glossary, a bibliography, and an index provide additional resources.

2 Has the Internet Made Bullying Worse?

Bullies can be found in many places. These include school cafeterias, the mall, and playgrounds. In recent years new technology has made a new place for bullies—the Internet. The Cyberbullying Research Center has looked at this issue. It says about 20 percent of students say they have been cyberbullied at some point in their lives. Youth culture has shifted from playgrounds to chat rooms. And the potential for bullying and its impact on those who are bullied has become much worse.

Easier Access to Victims

Raychelle Cassada Lohmann is the author of *The Anger Workbook for Teens*. She says the Internet has given teens

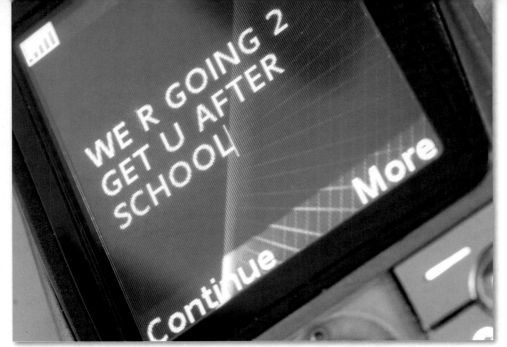

New technologies have given bullies easier access to their victims. They can send threatening e-mails, text messages, or instant messages.

many ways to bully. She says, "Young people can quickly spread a rumor through texting, taping an embarrassing incident and posting it on YouTube, or uploading pictures or unkind comments on social networking sites. There are many different avenues that can be used to cyberbully. . . . One wrong click has the power to change someone's life forever."[4] Lohmann also says that the Internet makes it easier to bully. Bullies can hide behind a computer screen or cell phone. She writes, "It's an easier way to bully because unlike traditional bullying it doesn't involve face to face interaction. Teens can become desensitized

Bullying is more widespread due to the Internet and cell phones. Victims no longer have a place to feel safe.

to a computer screen, and say or do things they wouldn't do to a person's face. The computer desensitizes teens and decreases the level of **empathy** they feel toward the victim. Plus, when they can't see the person's reaction to what they post or text they may not know if they've gone too far."[5]

No Place Is Safe

No place is safe from bullying on the Internet. Home is no longer a safe place. Bullies can reach victims anywhere and anytime through cell phones, the Internet, and social media. Natalie Farzaneh's problem with

Internet Amplifies Hurt

In 2003, 13-year-old Ryan Halligan committed suicide. He was being bullied by classmates in person and online. He was threatened, taunted, and insulted online many times. His father, John, says that the Internet made the bullying worse. In an interview for *Frontline*, John Halligan says:

> The computer and the Internet were not the cause of my son's suicide, but I believe they helped amplify and accelerate the hurt and the pain that he was trying to deal with that started at school and in person in the real world. . . . I think every time you log in to the Internet, you should be identified. When you go out into the world physically, people see you. When you do stuff, they see you. When you say something, they know it's coming from you. When you write something and send it into a newspaper, they won't print a letter to the editor without confirming that indeed it came from you and that you are who you say you are. On the Internet, I think you have to have that same kind of traceability, that same accountability,

Frontline, "Interviews: John Halligan," PBS.org, 2008.

bullying was made worse by the Internet. The half-Iranian teen says that she was targeted at school by bullies who made fun of her weight and Middle Eastern looks. But at least when she went home, the bullying stopped and she felt safe. That changed when she joined a social networking site. She received messages online from people telling her to kill herself and that everyone hated her. Suddenly, she felt as if she had nowhere to hide from the bullying.

Reaching More People

Today bullies can spread harmful messages to hundreds of people in a few seconds online. "With cyberbullying, victims may feel they've been **denigrated** in front of a wider audience," says Mitch van Geel, the lead author of a study on cyberbullying. "[And material] can be stored online, which may cause victims to relive the denigrating experience more often."[6]

The Internet is a powerful tool. It has many benefits for society. But when bullies go online to torment and harass their victims, the Internet can be a dangerous place.

But Not So Fast....

 No: The Internet Has Not Made Bullying Worse

Bullying is not a new problem in society. Bullies and bullying existed long before the Internet. Cyberbullying is just another form of traditional bullying. The Cyberbullying Research Center says only about one in five teens has been cyberbullied at least once in his or her lifetime. About one in ten kids are bullied in a thirty-day time period. All bullying is a problem. But these numbers show that the Internet has not created a bullying **epidemic**.

Face-to-Face Bullying Is More Common

Bullying in person is still common. In fact, it takes place more often than cyberbullying among today's youth. Dan Olweus is a Swedish psychologist. He has spent more than 40 years doing research on bullying among kids. He says that his research proves that face-to-face bullying is more of a problem than cyberbullying.

A Minnesota teacher uses an Olweus bullying prevention talk to speak to students about bullying.

This type of bullying should be the focus of prevention programs. "Claims by the media and researchers that cyberbullying has increased dramatically . . . are largely exaggerated," says Olweus. "There is very little scientific support to show that cyberbullying has increased over the past five to six years."[7] He says this form of bullying takes place less often than traditional bullying.

Olweus has done many large studies with US students in grades three to twelve. He says about 18 percent of these students said they had been verbally bullied. But only about 5 percent said they had been cyberbullied. Other studies done in Norway found that 11 percent of students said they had been verbally bullied. But only 4 percent said they had been cyberbullied. "These results suggest that the new electronic media have actually created few 'new' victims and bullies," Olweus says. "To be cyberbullied or to cyberbully other students seems to a large extent to be part of a general pattern of bullying where use of electronic media is only one possible form, and, in addition, a form with low prevalence."[8]

Face-to-Face Bullying Is Crueler than Cyberbullying

Many victims of bullying say that bullying in person is worse than cyberbullying. In person, they cannot just walk away. And they cannot block the bully like they can online.

In 2015 the Queensland University of Technology in Australia did a study. It found that most students think bullying in person is more harsh and cruel than cyberbullying. For the study, 156 students were asked about their views on being bullied. Fifty-nine percent of the students said bullying in person is worse than cyberbullying. Twenty-six percent said the two types of

Exaggerated Reports Increase Bullying Risk

The media sometimes exaggerates news reports of cyberbullying. This can have a negative effect. It can increase the actual bullying risk. Larry Magid writes about Internet safety. He says that the news media must report accurate rates and not exaggerate a behavior that is not common. He writes:

> Putting the bullying problem into its proper perspective doesn't minimize it, but actually helps prevent it from getting worse. There is a lot of solid research that shows that if people overestimate anti-social or harmful behavior, they are more likely to engage in it themselves. In other words, reporting accurately about the rate of bullying actually makes kids less likely to bully others. . . . To put it simply, overestimating bullying makes it seem like it's common.

Larry Magid, "Exaggerating Bullying Could Increase Bullying," *Huffington Post,* October 26, 2011. www.huffingtonpost.com.

Recent studies have found that incidents of face-to-face bullying far exceed those of cyberbullying.

bullying are equally harmful. And only 15 percent said they think cyberbullying is worse. The study concluded that being physically close during face-to-face bullying makes it more harsh than online bullying.

Media Exaggeration

Some think that cyberbullying has become an epidemic. This idea may be linked to news stories on high-profile cases. Anne Collier is co-director of the website *ConnectSafely.org*. She thinks that the media has created the false idea that a cyberbullying epidemic exists. She writes:

There is no cyberbullying epidemic. . . . I can't believe how many times I've been asked about "the epidemic" and what's to be done about it. . . . We've been experiencing an epidemic of *news coverage* of cyberbullying. We have *got* to be able to make the distinction between our children's experiences and what news stories seem to be saying about our children's experiences. If 80% of children have "not" experienced cyberbullying, is cyberbullying an epidemic? I think not.[9]

Closing Arguments

Most people agree that bullying is an issue. It does not matter whether it takes place in person or over the Internet. Some people say that the Internet has increased bullying's harmful effects. Others say that it is still just a small part of a larger bullying problem. As technology continues to change and bullies adapt their behaviors, the debate will continue.

Examine the Opinions

Understanding Primary and Secondary Sources

The author of this book uses a variety of sources to enhance the text. These sources are cited near the end of this book under the section Notes. The notes contain both primary and secondary sources. Learning the difference between these sources is important when writing an essay, or reading articles and studies. The basic difference is that primary sources are firsthand sources—people who were at an event and are conveying their impressions of that event. Secondary sources are second hand impressions—recalling or taking and using the opinions of others to produce a work about the event.

Primary sources include diaries, letters, memoirs, speeches, editorials, and interviews. They can also be newspaper or magazine articles if they cover an event while it is happening. In addition, photographs, audio and video recordings, research reports and studies, and literary works are also considered primary sources. Secondary sources interpret events using primary sources.

Examples can include biographies, histories, textbooks, encyclopedias, and reference books. Both types of sources are valuable to the researcher. For example, a primary source such as the text of a speech by Martin Luther King, Jr. would allow a researcher to experience the artistry of his words. But a secondary source such as a commentary on the speech and how it was accepted at the time would allow a researcher to gain an understanding of the context of the speech.

Using the notes and the information provided, a few of the sources would be categorized this way:

Notes 4 and 5 quote the author of a book called *The Anger Workbook for Teens*. The quote is taken from an article on bullying in *Psychology Today*. This is an example of a secondary source.

Note 6 quotes Mitch van Geel, the author of a study on cyberbullying. While Mitch van Geel's study might be considered a primary source, this quote is taken from a secondary source, a website that is reporting on the study.

In addition, the two sidebars in this chapter also use sources. The first quotes an interview of a father whose son committed suicide after being cyberbullied, which is a primary source. As you read throughout this book, try to determine whether other quotes are primary or secondary sources.

3 Are Schools Doing Enough to Stop Bullying?

 Yes: Schools Are Doing Enough to Stop Bullying

The National Center for Education Statistics says nearly one-third of school-age youth are bullied each year. Bullying can have serious consequences. These include an increased risk for depression and anxiety. Victims can have sleep problems. And they can do poorly in school. In order to protect all students, many schools have taken a leading role in the fight against bullying. Most schools have put anti-bullying programs in place. These help teach students and staff about bullying issues and improve the school atmosphere.

Middle school principal Miguel Salazar walks among some seventh graders during their lunch period. The school adopted the Olweus Bullying Prevention Program to help in the prevention and elimination of bullying in their school.

Anti-bullying Program Success

At Sunset Ridge Middle School in Salt Lake City, Utah, an anti-bullying program uses student **ambassadors**. They help spread anti-bullying messages and strategies in the school. Julie Scherzinger is a counselor at the school. She says that using students as ambassadors to spread these messages works well. It works better than having adults talk to kids about bullying. And it is easier for kids to report a problem to another student. The school's program focuses on different aspects of bullying. It uses themes of showing respect and empathy. It also stresses accepting many kinds of people. "We spend four or five months talking about different types of bullying and how not to get caught up in that and how to prevent it," Scherzinger says. "Then we spend January through May focusing on, 'this is what we want to see happen now.'"[10]

The program teaches kids to take the lead in preventing bullying. One student had a sticky note placed on her back that made fun of her weight. "It devastated the student. She was very upset," says Scherzinger. More than 1,000 students responded by wearing sticky notes to school that read, "Not in Our School." This is the name of their anti-bullying program. The program has worked so well that it is being rolled out to more schools in the district. "We are seeing [bullying] younger and younger and that's why the elementaries have asked us to come in and share our message and empower other students so that they know that they can stop it,"[11] Scherzinger says.

Laws and Policies to Prevent Bullying

All US states except Montana have anti-bullying laws or policies in place. These require schools to take steps to stop bullying, like the program at Sunset Ridge. These steps include anti-bullying practices and courses. They also include school procedures for reporting and looking into bullying.

Many schools throughout the United States are adopting anti-bullying policies.

In 2011 New Jersey governor Chris Christie signed a new law. It is one of the country's toughest anti-bullying laws. The law sets procedures for students and schools to report, investigate, and resolve bullying instances. "This act will help to reduce the risk of suicide among students and avert not only the needless loss of a young life, but also the tragedy that such loss represents to the student's family and the community at large,"[12] the law reads.

Schools Cannot Prevent Bullying Off Campus

When bullying takes place off campus or online, schools may not be able to do as much. Mark Crawford is superintendent of New York's West Seneca Schools. He says that cyberbullying is hard for schools to deal with. "We don't have the legal authority to intervene in a situation which exists between one child's computer and another child's computer when they are not being supervised when they are off school grounds," says Crawford. "But that doesn't mean we don't care . . . and it doesn't mean we don't make efforts to intervene when we can."[13]

Taking Anti-bullying Messages Onstage

Some schools are taking a creative approach to spread and reinforce anti-bullying messages to students. Lanny Sorenson is a theater teacher at Sunset Ridge Middle School in Salt Lake City, Utah. He stages plays that include real-life bullying encountered by students at his school. The middle school students submit stories about bullying that they experienced or saw. Sorenson takes these stories and puts them into a play. His goal is for the play to end with a message of hope. Each play is put on by as many as 90 student actors. The play's message is strong and has been an effective tool to combat bullying. "When it's kids talking about their own specific experiences, then kids tend to listen to each other," Sorenson says. He says that students are more likely to pay attention to the play's anti-bullying message because it comes directly from their peers.

Quoted in Andrew Adams, "Successful Anti-bully Program Expands," KSL. com, August 8, 2013.

Schools are making efforts to prevent bullying on school grounds. But they cannot police students 24 hours a day. Instead, the most effective bullying prevention begins at home. Parents must teach their kids about bullying issues before schools even get involved.

But Not So Fast....

Schools could be doing much more when it comes to preventing bullying. Many schools say they have anti-bullying policies and programs. But many of these are not being properly enforced. As a result, bullying continues, and schools are not a safe place for all students.

Lack of Enforcement

Anti-bullying policies do not work if they are not enforced. The Renaissance Charter School is in Port St. Lucie, Florida. It is being investigated for not following anti-bullying policies. Ten-year-old Cody Geissler went to the school for three years. He has ADHD and a form of autism called Asperger's. His mother, Amber, says that his classmates bullied him. She says that the bullies would corner him in the bathroom, shove him against the wall, throw things at him, and trip him. Amber says that she repeatedly reported the bullying to her son's teachers, school counselors, and administrators.

Demonstrators march to bring awareness of bullying in schools. Some schools are not properly enforcing state anti-bullying laws.

Florida law says that schools must look into bullying complaints. Schools must also report all incidents of bullying. But Renaissance did not report a single case of bullying during the 2009–2010 or 2010–2011 school years, even though Amber told school officials her son was being bullied.

Questionable Results

Some schools do follow anti-bullying procedures. But even in these schools, the programs may not work to reduce bullying. New Jersey did a survey of school administrators in 2012. It found that 41 percent were not sure if the state's new anti-bullying policies were effective. More than 29 percent said that new anti-bullying programs did not seem to improve civility in their schools or reduce bullying.

Bullying Prevention Begins at Home

Schools play a role in bullying prevention. But parents are a stronger influence on bullying behavior. Steve Siebold is an author and critical thinking expert. He believes that parents need to teach their kids not to bully. He writes:

> Parents need to be more involved with their children, and stop bullying in its tracks. If not, parents need to be held accountable, too. There's no excuse for roughly 160,000 kids a day cowering in terror. The blame rests on the shoulders of the leaders we trust to keep our kids safe, and on all parents to be more involved and teach their kids to treat others like they would like to be treated.

Steve Siebold, "Parents Should Be Charged Along with Kids in Bullying Cases," *Huffington Post*, October 21, 2013. www.huffingtonpost.com.

Zero-Tolerance Policies Do Not Work

Many school bullying incidents have led to violence. These include the shootings at Columbine High School. Some US schools have put zero-tolerance bullying policies in place. They apply a strict and severe punishment such as suspending a child from school for bullying. It does not matter why the bullying took place. But, such policies do not solve the bullying problem. Instead they just lead to more punishment without looking at why bullying occurs or how to change it. Also, the threat of severe punishment may deter kids and adults from reporting bullying that they see.

In some cases zero-tolerance policies prevent students from standing up to bullies. Nine-year-old Nathan Pemberton was kicked and punched by bullies. He fought back. And he was suspended from his elementary school. Stormy Rich was a high school student in Umatilla, Florida. She saw several students bullying a mentally challenged student on the school bus. Rich reported the bullying to the bus driver and the school. But the bullying continued. It looked like the school was not going to do anything about

While some schools have adopted zero-tolerance policies for bullying, many do not know exactly how to implement the policies.

the bullying. Rich told the bullies that she would step in if they did not stop bullying the girl. The school sent Rich's mom a letter that called Rich a bully for telling the girls to stop. And Rich was banned from riding the school bus.

Uncertainty Off Campus

Many schools are often not sure what to do when bullying takes place off campus or online. More and more bullying takes place online. Many states, cities, and parents want schools to adopt anti-cyberbullying policies and programs. Yet schools have little guidance or funding to do so. John R. Nodecker is the assistant superintendent of Pennsylvania's Hatboro-Horsham School District. He says, "There's a confusion to the entire situation." He says school leaders are left "in a kind of place where every situation seems like a test case."[14]

Closing Arguments

Preventing bullying is the goal of students, parents, and schools. To do this, many schools use a variety of programs. These are meant to teach kids and staff about bullying. They also aim to reduce bullying behaviors. For some people, these are not enough. They say that schools need better enforcement of their anti-bullying policies and better programs to reduce bullying. As long as bullying continues to occur, the issue will continue to be debated.

Examine the Opinions

Bias

In this chapter, the author of the two essays uses **bias** when discussing the school's role in preventing bullying. *Bias* means having a strong opinion toward something. Bias can be negative or positive. It is important to be aware of a person's bias and take it into account.

In the first essay in the chapter, the author says that schools are doing all they can to stop bullying. She gives examples and quotes sources that agree that schools are doing everything they can. In the second essay, the author has the opposite bias. She says that schools are not doing enough to prevent bullying. She gives examples and quotes that agree with her position. Having a bias is not bad. We all have biases. Some are based on our experience. Some are just opinions that we have formed. But when forming your own opinion, it is important to see a person's bias and take it into account.

4 Should Bullying Be a Criminal Offense?

 Yes: Bullying Is a Crime and Should Be Prosecuted

In 2010 Phoebe Prince was a fifteen-year-old high school freshman in South Hadley, Massachusetts. She was repeatedly bullied by a group of classmates for several months. As a result, she hung herself from a stairwell in her home. Elizabeth Scheibel is a district attorney in the state. She announced **felony indictments** against six teens for their role in Prince's bullying and suicide. Eventually, five of the teens agreed to plea deals on misdemeanor charges. They were sentenced to probation and community service. Charges against the sixth teen were dropped.

District attorney Elizabeth Scheibel announces felony indictments against six teens for their role in the 2010 bullying and subsequent suicide of Phoebe Prince.

Damaging Form of Abuse

At one time, bullying was thought to be a rite of passage. Today parents, schools, and communities see bullying as a damaging form of abuse. It can have long-lasting, serious consequences for victims. Like other forms of abuse, bullying is a crime. It should be prosecuted to the fullest.

In addition, criminal charges in bullying cases can serve a purpose. They can deter bullying behavior.

Richard Cole is a lawyer and school safety consultant. He says that even though no one went to jail, the Prince case sent a strong message that bullying is a crime that will not be tolerated. Cole says that the case "definitely acts as a deterrent to others." He adds, "There absolutely are times when you need to get the criminal justice system involved."[15]

Need for Improved Laws

Some states and cities recognize that bullying is a crime that should be prosecuted. They are making their anti-bullying laws stronger. And they are adding specific penalties for bullying and cyberbullying. In Florida, lawmakers have proposed Rebecca's Law. It calls for bullying to be a criminal offense. The proposed law is named after Rebecca Sedwick. She was a 12-year-old who committed suicide in 2013 after being bullied by peers. Punishments under the proposed law vary. They could include a fine or jail time. Florida state representative Heather Fitzenhagen is a sponsor of the bill. She hopes that if the bill passes, it will bring more

In 2013 the suicide of 12-year-old Rebecca Sedwick prompted an anti-bullying law in the Florida legislature.

attention to bullying as a criminal offense across the nation. She hopes the bill will lead people to talk about bullying at home and in schools. "I think this is going to raise awareness because now there is a consequence to this type of behavior,"[16] she says.

In 2015, Colorado voted on a bill that would make cyberbullying a crime. The bill changes the state's harassment laws to specifically address cyberbullying.

Keeping Laws Up to Date with Technology

The Internet and new digital technologies keep growing and changing. And they have given bullies new ways to torment their victims. Jeffrey Klein, a state senator from New York, believes that new laws are needed to make cyberbullying a crime. He says:

> Our laws are not keeping pace with technology, and we are paying a human price for it. No longer is bullying only confined to the schoolyard, it is now piped in an instant through victims' computers and onto the devices they carry in their pockets. This legislation will help provide protections to those who need it, as well as send a strong message about the seriousness of this destructive behavior.

Quoted in Dominique Debucquoy-Dodley, "New York Looks to 'Modernize' Cyberbullying Laws," CNN.com, September 27, 2011.

Those found guilty of cyberbullying face jail or a fine. Supporters say that it is needed to send a message that cyberbullying can have severe consequences and will not be tolerated in the state.

But Not So Fast.....

Bullying should not be tolerated. But passing new laws to make it a crime is not the answer. Bullying is hurtful and cruel. But it is not a crime. Sometimes bullying crosses the line and involves invasion of privacy, harassment, or stalking. Then existing laws can be used to prosecute offenders. Eli Federman is a law school graduate. He says that attempts to make bullying a crime are off base. He says they are an overreaction to recent cases in which bullied teens have committed suicide. He writes, "While there should be zero tolerance for bullying, criminalizing the behavior is not the answer."[17] If a bully's actions cannot be prosecuted under existing laws, then they are not a crime.

Violating Free-Speech Rights

Making bullying a crime may be **unconstitutional**. The First Amendment gives all US citizens freedom of

Several anti-bullying laws violate free-speech rights.

speech. The courts have overturned several anti-bullying laws. These laws violated free-speech rights.

In 2014 the New York State Court of Appeals struck down a law that made cyberbullying a crime. The law was passed in 2010 after an Albany teen made a Facebook page to embarrass and harass classmates. The court ruled that the law was too broad. It violated the free-speech rights of online bullies. The court said, "Although the First Amendment may not give the defendant the right to engage in these activities, the text of Albany County's law envelops far more than acts of cyberbullying against children by criminalizing a variety of constitutionally protected modes of expression."[18] Corey Stoughton was the lead attorney on the case. He agrees with the court's decision. "Cyberbullying is a serious concern that all communities must confront, but there are better and more constructive ways to address the problem than giving children criminal records,"[19] he says. He adds that doing so does not get at the root of bullying or stop it from taking place.

Not an Effective Deterrent

The threat of criminal charges may lead bullies to become better at hiding their acts. "Criminalizing these behaviors is not going to be the most effective thing to prevent them,"[20] says Elizabeth Englander. She is director of the Massachusetts Aggression Reduction Center. She says that it is hard to know whether the threat of criminal charges will stop bullying. It may just drive bullies underground.

Bullying Laws Are Unconstitutional

In 2014 a proposed law to make bullying a crime was struck down in Colorado. People against the law said that it violated free-speech rights. Eugene Volokh is a professor at the UCLA School of Law. Mike Krause is director of the Justice Policy Initiative at the Independence Institute. The two wrote a letter to the Colorado Senate to say they were opposed to the bill. They wrote:

> We realize that people are worried about teenagers taunting one another online. In a few situations, such taunting has contributed to teenagers' suicide. But we're not sure there's any way of clearly defining which distressing speech about minors should be criminal and which shouldn't be.
>
> This statute surely doesn't offer any such distinction. It isn't limited to speech *to* a person . . . but also covers speech *about* a person. . . . It even covers speech on publicly significant topics, as well as speech about people's daily lives.

Eugene Volokh and Mike Krause, "Colorado Senate Should Kill Cyberbullying Bill That Violates Free Speech," *Denver Post*, March 21, 2014.

A Better Way: Changing School Atmosphere

A better way to stop bullying is a change to the school atmosphere. Schools should create an environment where students and staff view bullying as unacceptable. In order to do this, both students and staff should be included in the process. The Anoka-Hennepin School District near Minneapolis wanted to deal with bullying that led to several student suicides. It created focus groups of students. The groups came up with ideas of what schools, teachers, and other students could do to make bullying no longer tolerated in their schools. Teachers and staff are

Students are encouraged to make recommendations for what administrators, teachers, and other students can do to no longer tolerate bullying in their schools.

being trained to stop bullying. And students are giving feedback on how it is working. Ann Lindsey is a middle school teacher in the district. She says the efforts are working and that her school's atmosphere has changed a lot. "I'm thrilled to say students can walk through the halls and feel safe," she says. "The mood is much brighter; the slurs have decreased."[21]

Closing Arguments

Bullying can have serious, long-lasting consequences. Some people say that making bullying a crime with serious penalties will make bullies think twice before hurting others. Others disagree. They say that there are better ways to stop bullying than dragging kids through the legal system. Whether bullying should be prosecuted as a crime remains an issue.

Examine the Opinions

Testimonials

In this chapter, the author quotes lawyers and other professionals who deal with bullying issues. They give their opinions about bullying as a crime. One of these is lawyer Corey Stoughton. He thinks that bullying should not be a crime. He says that laws against cyberbullying violate free-speech rights. When a writer quotes an expert, it is called a testimonial. A testimonial offers further evidence or proof of an opinion. When evaluating a testimonial, it is important to look at the source. Is the source an expert in the subject? Is he or she part of a group that is an authority on the subject? On the other hand, is the source biased about the topic? Does he or she have something to gain by supporting one side of an issue? Looking at the source will help you decide how reliable the testimonial is. It is important to keep in mind that an expert's opinion can be biased. For instance, a person who works for a group such as Greenpeace will hold certain views about the environment. A person affected by a certain disease may also be biased. This does not make his or her opinion unworthy of consideration. But it is important to know the person's bias and take that into account.

Wrap It Up!

In this book, the author gave many opinions about bullying. These can be used to write a short essay on bullying. Short opinion essays are a common writing form. They are also a good way to use the ideas in this book. The author gave many common argumentative techniques and evidence that can be used. Quoting from primary and/or secondary sources, bias, and testimonials were argumentation techniques used in the essays to sway the reader. Any of these could be used in a piece of writing.

There are 6 steps to follow when writing an essay:

Step One: Choose a Topic

When writing your essay, first choose a topic. You can start with one of the three chapter questions from the table of contents in this book.

Step Two: Choose Your Theme

Decide which side of the issue you will take. After choosing your topic, use the materials in this book to write the thesis, or theme, of your essay. You can use the titles of the articles in this book or the sidebar titles as examples of themes. The first paragraph should state your theme. For example, in an essay titled "Excluding Students from Online Groups Is Not Bullying," state your opinion. Say why you think excluding others online is not bullying even though it can hurt their feelings. You could also use a short anecdote, or story, that proves your point and will interest your reader.

Step Three: Research Your Topic

You will need to do some further research to find enough material for your topic. You can find useful books and articles to look up in the bibliography and the notes of this book. Be sure to cite your sources, using the notes at the back of this book as an example.

Step Four: The Body of the Essay

In the next three paragraphs, develop this theme. To develop your essay, come up with three reasons why excluding others online is not bullying. For instance, three reasons could be:

- The Internet is increasingly being used to organize social outings.
- It is unrealistic to expect everyone to be friends.
- Just because someone's feelings are hurt doesn't mean that bullying has occurred.

These three ideas should each be given their own paragraph. Be sure to give a piece of evidence in each paragraph. This could be a testimonial from a teen who uses the Internet to plan a night at the movies. Each paragraph should end with a transition sentence that sums up the main idea in the paragraph and moves the reader to the next one.

Step Five: Write the Conclusion

The final, or fifth, paragraph should state your conclusion. This should restate your theme and sum up the ideas in your essay. It could also end with an engaging quote or piece of evidence that wraps up your essay.

Step Six: Review Your Work

Finally, be sure to reread your essay. Does it have quotes, facts, and/or anecdotes to support the conclusions? Are the ideas clearly presented? Have another reader take a look at it to see if someone else can understand your ideas. Make any changes that you think can help make your essay better.

Congratulations on using the ideas in this book to write a personal essay!

Notes

Chapter 1: The Bullying Problem

1. Quoted in CBS News, "Bullying: Words Can Kill," September 23, 2013. www.cbsnews.com.
2. Quoted in CBS News, "Bullying."
3. Quoted in CBS News, "Bullying."

Chapter 2: Has the Internet Made Bullying Worse?

4. Raychelle Cassada Lohmann, "Cyberbullying Versus Traditional Bullying," *Teen Angst* (blog), *Psychology Today*, May 14, 2012. www.psychologytoday.com.
5. Lohmann, "Cyberbullying Versus Traditional Bullying."
6. Quoted in Sy Mukherjee, "Study: Kids Who Are Cyberbullied Are 3 Times More Likely to Contemplate Suicide," ThinkProgress, March 11, 2014. http://thinkprogress.org.
7. Quoted in American Psychological Association, "Cyberbullying Less Frequent than Traditional Bullying, According to International Studies," August 4, 2012. www.apa.org.
8. Quoted in American Psychological Association, "Cyberbullying Less Frequent than Traditional Bullying, According to International Studies."
9. Ann Collier, "A Cyberbullying Epidemic? No!" Net Family News, July 19, 2011. www.netfamilynews.org.

Chapter 3: Are Schools Doing Enough to Stop Bullying?

10. Quoted in Paul Nelson, "Students Taking Ownership of Anti-bullying Program," KSL.com, January 17, 2013. www.ksl.com.

11. Quoted in Andrew Adams, "Successful Anti-bully Program Expands," KSL.com, August 8, 2013. www.ksl.com.
12. Quoted in Emmeline Zhao, "New Jersey's Anti-bullying Law, Toughest in Country, Garners Praise and Criticism," *Huffington Post*, September 2, 2011. www.huffingtonpost.com.
13. Quoted in Dave McKinley, "Are Schools Doing Enough to Prevent Bullying?" WGRZ.com, September 22, 2011. http://amherst.wgrz.com.
14. Quoted in Michelle Davis, "Schools Tackle Legal Twists and Turns of Cyberbullying," *Education Week*, February 4, 2011.

Chapter 4: Should Bullying Be a Criminal Offense?

15. Quoted in Greg Toppo, "Should Bullies Be Treated as Criminals?" *USA Today*, June 13, 2012.
16. Quoted in Julie Dahl, "Rebecca's Law Aims to Punish Bullying in Fla." CBS News, January 17, 2014.
17. Eli Federman, "Bullying Is Bad, but Criminalizing Bullying Would Be Even Worse," *Forbes*, October 23, 2013.
18. Quoted in Aaron Short, "Cyberbullies Get First Amendment Protection," *New York Post*, July 1, 2014.
19. Quoted in Short, "Cyberbullies Get First Amendment Protection."
20. Quoted in Toppo, "Should Bullies Be Treated as Criminals?"
21. Quoted in Maggie Clark, "Criminal Case Puts Focus on Bullying Laws," Pew Charitable Trusts, November 4, 2013. www.pewresearch.org.

Glossary

ambassadors: People who represent a group or promote a specific activity.

bias: A strong opinion about something.

denigrated: Criticized, belittled, or attacked verbally.

empathy: The ability to understand the feelings of other people.

epidemic: A widespread occurrence of a problem in a community at a particular time.

felony: A crime punishable by death or more than one year in jail.

indictments: Formal charges of a serious crime.

unconstitutional: Not in accordance with the US Constitution.

Bibliography

Books

David M. Haugen, *Bullying*. Detroit: Greenhaven, 2014.

Rachel Stuckey, *Cyber Bullying*. New York: Crabtree, 2013.

Mathangi Subramania, *Bullying: The Ultimate Teen Guide*. Lanham, MD: Rowman & Littlefield, 2014.

Articles

CBS News, "Bullying: Words Can Kill," September 23, 2013. www.cbsnews.com.

Maggie Clark, "Criminal Case Puts Focus on Bullying Laws," Pew Charitable Trusts, November 4, 2013. www.pewtrusts.org.

Michelle Davis, "Schools Tackle Legal Twists and Turns of Cyberbullying," *Education Week*, February 4, 2011. www.edweek.org.

Websites

Cyberbullying Research Center (http://cyberbullying.us). This website has information and links to cyberbullying information, facts, and resources for students, parents, and educators.

National Bullying Prevention Center (www.pacer.org/bullying). The National Bullying Prevention Center works to make bullying no longer accepted as a childhood rite of passage. The website provides resources for students, parents, and educators, and includes educational toolkits, awareness toolkits, contest ideas, promotional products, and more.

StopBullying.gov (www.stopbullying.gov). This federal government website is managed by the US Department of Health and Human Services. It offers information, facts, and resources about bullying and cyberbullying.

Index

About the Author

Carla Mooney is an author of many books for young readers. She loves learning about issues and understanding different opinions. A graduate of the University of Pennsylvania, she lives in Pittsburgh, Pennsylvania, with her husband and three children.